FREEDOM HOUSE

FREEDOM HOUSE

Poems

KB Brookins

DEEP
VELLUM

Deep Vellum Publishing
3000 Commerce St., Dallas, Texas 75226
deepvellum.org · @deepvellum

Deep Vellum is a 501c3 nonprofit literary arts organization
founded in 2013 with the mission to bring
the world into conversation through literature.

ISBNs: 9781646052639 (paperback) | 9781646052844 (ebook)

Library Of Congress Control Number: 2023002917

Support for this publication has been provided in part by the National Endowment for the Arts, the Texas Commission on the Arts, the City of Dallas Office of Arts and Culture, and the George and Fay Young Foundation

Cover design by Zoe Norvell | Cover photograph by Denise Andersen (via Shutterstock)
Typesetting by www.INeedABookInterior.com

Printed in the United States of America

Also by KB Brookins:

How to Identify Yourself with a Wound

"I believe in transformation, and for the first time in my life, I really get how transformation is impossible without honest acceptance of who you are, whence you came, what you do in the dark, and how you want to love and be loved tomorrow."

—KIESE LAYMON

"I thought I was gon' write a rap but this be baby miracle."

—NONAME

TABLE OF CONTENTS

BLACK LIFE CIRCA 2029

Clean fridge.
Spacious, carpeted living room.
Newly swept floors. A wooden desk. Designated
lunchtime every day at noon.
SZA playing on vinyl.
Window blinds, open & intact.
Money, crisp & resting in the bank.
Sour gummy worms with wine on the counter.

        I visit my mother regularly & tell her I love her.
        I don't flinch when my father raises his arm.
        My father raises his arm to hug me.
        The hood walks me, & sometimes, I walk it back.
        The hood is a small utopia of green grass.
        All the Cadillacs are Barbie-painted.
        I walk the eastside & don't get hit on.
        Black men gleam gold teeth, & there are no police.

I go up the street to eat, & there are no police.
The Black boy shoots a toy gun; still, no police.
There are no police at the school or hiding behind
exit signs on the freeway. I don't clutch my
steering wheel when black-and-white cars appear close.
I don't get handcuffed or questioned—my lover doesn't
have to hold me. Handcuffs exist only for the filthiest
of kink shit; I don't have to call in *Black* the next day.

        I don't replay the night in my head. The ticket
        doesn't get paid off; there isn't a target on my back
        that I can't remove. There isn't a target on my face
        when I cry at night, or in the morning, or in the restroom
        during my designated lunch, closer to 12:30.
        I love my land, comfortable; I love this life, loud.
        I have a living—
        I have a room.

I. FOYER

KB'S ORIGIN STORY

I was born a weary son
painted into a family unit. I can't
fit in, but I do fit jeans if I squeeze
enough. I pain myself
with laughter when someone asks
whose baby is this. I sleep
in a tunnel of judgments I can't kick.
I was born a drury daughter
crashed into a tiny parked car. In the impact
my feelings sprawl all over
the navy leather passenger seat.
This can't be a wonderful scene:
the navy leather passenger seat
& my feelings sprawled all over.
A tiny parked car crashes; in the impact,
I was born a drury daughter.
In a tunnel of judgments I can't kick,
I sleep. *Whose baby is this.*
With laughter, when someone asks
enough, I pain myself
to fit in. & I do fit genes if I squeeze
paint into a family unit. I can't
be born a weary son.

T SHOT #1

I feel my most alive when I'm the bearer of my own pain.
When I shift, squirm, & brace; when I plunge it in the gum

of me to feel. I pass over my ID. I peer
into what calls itself
controlled. Joy lives in such a little container. It sticks into
my muscle, emits a sweet, oily lifeline breathing

into slim rubber. I will not die, I promise you this. Even if
the bruise turns blue & creates a pretty palace on my skin,

on the other side of that flesh wall I am becoming
my own best man. Bring in the broom & bride.
Let the church bells breathe in liberty.

EVERY BUILDING IN EAST AUSTIN IS A GHOST

There isn't much that I know about this place, except
that every building is a ghost. Traveling, I find home

in bathrooms, buildings, people—yet here it sits
       in the sick of willful ignorance.
You see that bodega? It used to be a family tire shop.

You visit that coffee spot? It was made
       with rubbish of a 70-year-old home.
There's a scarcity of love built into all the asphalt.

Preservation depends on what is considered
       good. The city natives know still spills
in cracked corners of my local Whole Foods. I'm expected

to unsee that resurrection. Does no one else see mummies
       lost here? The local paper's business section
is an obituary. *We'll be building*

on top of your memory now. I don't know much
       about place, except that history is epistolary
& fresh paint is sometimes mixed with blood.

Heaven be a Rosewood Park Juneteenth.
Hell be a rent increase by property tax.

& SOMEHOW, MEN ARE NICER TO ME NOW

They say "hey boss" at me in restaurants. They hand me the check,
ask me about the game of Who vs Cares, give me tips
on how to talk to women tangential from the bar.
I wonder what about me makes them chipper & chatting
thinly about interestless shit; is it chestlessness? The disappearance
of my hourglass figure? The chin hair, stubby & manly as livers
drowning under kegs of cheap craft beer? They tell me

not to drink fruity shit tonight. Like yesterday,
when I couldn't get any investment in my breath so a cop
wrestled me to the stiff concrete, didn't happen. Like everything
I've lived through isn't etched in the beard they tell me to marinate in oils.
It'll grow, bro they say. Every man treats me like I'm living
now. Somehow, when this life is over, I will have lived both sides
of the offensive line—throw me the ball, fam. I'll be sure
to run into a teammate, tell them how men
are the silliest thing since touchdowns were invented.

SEXTING AT THE GYNECOLOGIST

A camera is what makes it porn right? I google as everyone
in the reception area wonders what husband is waiting for his wife.

Between my legs is a national treasure or at least what gives
republicans wet dreams during seasons of political theater. Can I carry

that energy into a pose that reads *digital exchange of chemistry*? The tiny
bathroom mirror says yes. My lover opens the text as some other kind of camera

enters the canal that never wanted this. The same way republicans
never want their donors to think they care about trans people. If I blur

the silhouette, is it still considered erotica? I think so,
said the nurse answering a separate question about my womb. If cameras

create the crime then I declare my pants untenable by white people
unless they're doing routine checkups in a doctor's office. At least here,

the lobby thinks I'm offering moral support. & in a way, tea & a backrub
says everything's okay just as much as my lover, eyes spangled

when I show her what Dan Patrick hates.

DINNER WITH JOHN CENA ON THE MOON

We start with him asking questions about my hair. How it
manages to move without thinking; I tell him *magic*, ask
him about having gnarled knuckles & a name that everyone
can recognize. He replies in simple yesnos; I sigh
in ways he doesn't recognize. I wonder if he views
his anger as himself. Though we live in light-years worth of orbit,
my diaphragm has never been so tense. His neck is long
& leaping in the direction of a crick. I say *hey* & he clinches
in resistance. He wonders if difference in muscle mass
helps a human land on a spaceship floor—I sit & he
floats, trembling. We both have a hard time saying how we feel.
We both hatewatch salisbury coating the axis of a planet
we can no longer see. I want to feel anger if it means landing
soon. He wants to live in relative obscurity if it means never
being this vulnerable again. *Are you happy with your job?*
I ask. *Are you happy, ever?* he whispers as sadness
withers the moon like gravity.

IT'S 6 AM & THE SUN IS OUT

I make peace with this being a beginning:
speaking
when commentary makes me unbelieve
in my body / saying *No*
when asked if I found a church home
in my respective
shelter city / saying *Because*
they're not good people when asked why I don't attend
family functions / spreading the good word
of moving out
of a town you could never call home
If home is really where the heart should be
my heart is somewhere in Fort Worth, Texas
between sundry items at Ramey Market
or sinking in Kool-Aid at Madea's Down Home Cooking
I don't remember a time I wasn't lying
about how much something harmed me
I run with the opposite
of progress
every time my father speaks
Congress is no match
to the grave I lay my mind in
I'm making peace
with all of the I's in this poem
unfortunately being the speaker
& I am tired
of making peace with small
progress being a precursor
for my death
& ignoring the pleading for a/c
permeating through my clothes every time

a Texas summer gets hotter / I make peace
with all the living things around me shaking
my hand as if we'll make it
through this
unscarred & together
& the sun
is just a metaphor for my falling—

THE PICKUP COMES AT 6 AM

I used to have boobs but now I have skin. Wrinkled skin. Welted,
brownish skin. Skin that laughs at the hue of skin around it. I used to
have boobs but now I have you, lying on top of what used to be

shame. You breathe so clearly I feel it through your nostrils.
Gnarled tissue only gets smoother as age kisses it. Your knuckles
finagle me until I feel new. I want you breathing

on top of me at all times. I also want to take the trash out
& not have people perplexed about my new-ish skin. The naked
crape myrtles tell me it's okay. They don't see skin grafts

& tell me to put a shirt on
nor remind me what wrongness recognized looks like
atop the neighbor's nosy face. I want to make you into everything
I encounter: all the tender hugs & shower sweetness.

All validation that we are nothing
but poorly decorated blood-figures.

EVERYTHING'S TEMPORARY

after Morgan Parker

I think I got it right last night.
I met a girl at Highland's
& we danced to the touch
of our tongues & the 20
-something's struggle till
the lights came up & she ran away.
I figured it was the tequila's fault.

Or she didn't know my gender
& that's the beauty of LED's.
on the way home, I slur to strangers
while "Closing Time" blares
over low-quality intercoms.

I wish every week could be as blissful as this,
but I'm Black & queer & trans & can't
escape this. On weekends, I do what I want
because everything's temporary.
Black & queer & trans bodies, this body,
& my fly fit for the function next Saturday.

After I sell my life
to corporate America, I'm going dancing
with my guys, & I plan to find another
lovable lady to land
these crispy lips on
so we can bond over brokenness & fill
our voids with songs & saliva
I hope to waste another night on something,
anything
other than—

KB GOES HOME FOR THE HOLIDAYS

I draw the line at making my voice squeak
        pushing it back to higher registers.
I make the sand sink as I swiftly move
        my leg from one side to the other at
They will notice the facial hair;
        should I remove it? & doing it.
My pores & thighs have worked too hard
        for this. I shave, tell them *be back*
in 6 months & want to love my grandmother
        the way I already do too much.
I elegy the prickly bush getting flushed
        down the drain. What can I tell the sand
squished in between my toes
        now that I've moved the line back again?
My stomach earthquakes when uncle
        asks *who is this?* as I speak. I betray
myself to answer that question.

WHAT'S ON YOUR MIND, KB?

after Patti Labelle's appearance on the Tyra Banks Show

The poison ivy leading to a gentrified beer garden. The inkling of dignity I feel when I don't let a white woman patronize me. Patti had the right idea; *Why did you think I would eat paper?* and *Why do you think less of me?* are inches away from sameness. The message in *don't try me* is *not today or any day*, or is it *we need an intervention?* Invite your mother, her mother, the fathers that whittled you into this boldness. Tell them all that something isn't okay. Bring snacks & make an aftercare plan for harm that extends centuries. These are the things I think about, friend. My mind is saying jigs have been up—it's time up with thinking I am anything less & you are everything personified, everything to aspire to, till death do us & everything apart. Till every death is inevitable except what made you. I'm tired of you & your people asking me questions. I want the beer garden to be a beer garden, & for my thoughts to be sprinkles of whatever you think of since thinking, for you, is a luxury.

II.
DINING ROOM

SONIC SYMBOLISM

For Ma'Khia Bryant, After Björk & Brittany Rogers

Hair falls out of my beard
The only hair I need external support
to grow

Butts clench and unclench
Throats close necessary
pathways for air

& hearts close up too.
The baby, once a happy
couple's pact between each other &
the possibility of birthing a new
bloodline erases as

the baby closes up too. I listen to a Black girl
take her last breath
in a struggle between police
& history

& somethings in me—sanity,
life, stands of Black hair,
guttural reactions to sound & light—

die to make way
for the always-crowning & bloody birth
of rage—

BARE MINIMUM, OR TO-DO LIST FOR WHITE AMERICA

Clean up after yourself. Pick up
that book chile, you still got
a good back. Seek therapy.
Don't kill the creative in you.
Don't kill Black people. Get a job—
one that doesn't make you
a dictator. Take back 400 years
of overcontested leadership. Give thanks
to the futures you've stolen.
Give back what your people call
inheritance. Wash your hands; cut
the grass; don't kill Asian women.
Don't have what you call *bad days*.
Don't think that—due to fear planted
in the roots of your kin—you can't get rid
of yourself today. Get a job—
one that doesn't require blood from me.
I'm low on iron & desire to tell you
once again. Quit playing. There is a puddle
of blood you've shoved into a corner.
There is a mop and my people
wringed into a bucket of waste. I'll wait.

TATTLETALE

This country lied I mean told a story
'bout me. I'm sorry. He said
I am some nigga from the hood
that asks for too much, less than
70 years after integrating schools.
Less than 70 days after banning
books that tell folk he
segregated schools. She said I am a liar
I mean a tattletale cause I'm
telling you, but I'm TELLING YOU, mama,
they spent 400 years telling tales
'bout slavery. I mean that they sinning,
not me. Anything I've done, they did
more times 10. I can't believe [any
pronoun] telling tales 'bout me. Ain't
killing, erasing, or just plain old lying
a better word for it? Mamie,
You have to believe me.

I believe you. Say sorry.

Okay.

ARS POETICA WITH ELECTION RESULTS STILL IN LIMBO

after torrin a. greathouse

This morning, I got an entire toenail taken off while checking my phone for an update. While watching the numbers in 4 states stagnate I thought to text you, the person that I would choose if living in an alternate universe where being with anyone I desired was on the table. This poem could never be able to desire. It could only be a hand on my belly when I wake up with no knowledge that a part I once grew could be taken away forever. It takes 6 months to completely grow this toenail back. In that time, we could fight a pandemic, cry over a white girl hurling her history at me, tell time it doesn't define us, that difference doesn't define us; when I look into your eyes, I am looking into a universe where I was never wounded. I peer back in the only ways this body has learned; I never wanted this election. Instead, I want a bowl of messy takeout & a lip-touch with tongue involved that tells me that I matter. That we matter. I am nothing without the throat that sings in pain as the day breaks open like a fungus sent off for lab work.

                                        checking
          the numbers   I thought to text
          an alternate universe
This poem could never be   desire. It could only be
          knowledge   away forever.   6 months
                              we could

                                                            look
               into a universe   I peer back
                         Instead
                                        I am nothing

This morning, I got   taken   .

                              I could only be

          a   wounded
body   ;

T SHOT #4

A boy can be a river if you let him. One where everyone
has fun in his waters & survives the flood. A boy is tender
as a turtle running to water not long after birth
if you stop him from drying up so soon. Niggas die

too often 'round here. 'round here, a boy is pinkish
& left in the sun. I want to drink from a river of Blackness
for a second, or a lifetime & no Florida mist takes me
back to this dimension where boys don't get to be men.

I want the Black boy to be a river you can't name
even if you send sounds underwater. Even if you swim & only
come up to be reminded of breath & sunlight.
I want to sink into ecosystems where human beingness sets in—

discover his genius. Don't dam him till he's a pond
or tourist attraction, or another potential gasping for air
like fish flopping for standerbys to kick it back in. Let's dive
headfirst, America. I hear the Colorado is bottomless.

WE ARE OWED THIS
On the day that Derek Chauvin is indicted & we learn of another murder

The least they could do is put a white boy in handcuffs. Push his face

into dirt, make him eat verdicts till his tongue mistakes

tanginess for justice. The least the state could do was put a man

behind bars with taxpayers & public backlash. That is not the extent of this country's

dreams. If I was a bird, I'd be something like a pigeon-eagle mix.

Bold & funnylooking, arrogant & identifiable by the genes etched

in my ancestors' wounds. In this hope, I see babies happy with

no cops around to shoot up their dreams. In this dream, prisons

evaporate like a Dr. Doctor shot with garlic & cayenne. We are owed

a spicy, iced-down future at least. We are owed a playground & uncles

to sell loosies at any corner store. We are owed children who call for help

from adults. Death isn't a lesson learned; it is only an ending,

an opportunity to do nothing else. If I am destined to be the bird,

I'll pick up all my niggas for the years-delayed migration

to landscapes where Black people live. We are owed this, plus a trip

down memory lane. Back to a time when treks were voluntary & never by ocean.

GREEDY GHAZAL

Met a dope boy on Tinder with big hands and big dreams.
In a world full of scarcity, he owes greed.

I extend compassion with my touch. He chokes me,
& I can tell his cracked palms know greed.

Afterwards he's bashful, asks me if I like women.
I like whatever I can get; unlike him, I've never known greed.

He wants to work in tech; utters ebonics & code-speak
but no degree, no prestige in a city drunk on dough-greed.

That's fucked up I moan as I climb the mountain of him
to see punched walls & bedroom plants. I too grow greed.

Nice & slow is boring; he worries he's *becoming gay*.
I say call me back over. You know you want some mo' greed.

Silicon Hills is the name. Gentrification is the game.
Companies give us pennies & we blow greed.

This bedroom is the only place we own. I throw
back on his rage. No passion, no greed.

CURRICULUM VITAE

KB
pronouns: whatever will get me the job
corporatebody@gmail.com
Surveillance available upon request

PROFESSIONAL SUMMARY

Emerging professional well versed in being poor. Ready for the next opportunity to fight for my life.

EDUCATION

- » Terminal degree in terror, expected 2022
- » Blackness, 1995–present
- » Queer-adjacent university, 2013–2017
- » Trans-exclusionary high school, 2009–2013

FELLOWSHIPS & AWARDS

- » **Marked as alive during global embarrassment,** 2016–2020
- » **Lifetime achievement in most tokenable,** 2019
- » **Inaugural Fellow,** psychiatrist's office, 2020–2021
- » **Winner,** "still okay" award after scrolling through trending topics, June 2020
- » **Semifinalist,** trauma dump scholarship, October 2021

WORK EXPERIENCE

Cashier and other things I wasn't paid for
A to B Grocery Store
April 2020–August 2021

- » Managed to run from point A to point B in roads greased in butter
- » Heard "the nerve of some Black people" and didn't end customer's life
- » Got no hazard pay; compartmentalized for the sake of crummy monthly payment
- » Assisted (while dissociating) with placing customers outside my comfort zone
- » Executed tasks that pertained to the CEO's pockets
- » Suppressed everyone else

Person who cares
Anything University
August 2019–March 2020

- » Explicitly told not to care; cared anyways
- » Pitched innovative strategies to deceive students of any marginalized identity
- » Worked with staff and faculty currently using or considering despair as an alternative to This
- » Wrapped myself in bubble wrap since I'm so damn fragile

Activist
Feminist Nonprofit
June 2018–July 2019

- » Promoted, co-produced, and attended indoctrination meetings and events
- » Realized that an unburdened girl is a rich girl or a liar
- » Fermented the fright of Black people while trying to fight for abortions
- » Stared at a murder of crows outside of the courtroom every time murder was up for senate bill number whatever

BOARD & COMMITTEE POSITIONS

» **Secretary**, Texas Climate Crisis Brigade, February 2021

» **Co-Chair,** Committee of Black people Who Survived, June 2020

» **Chair Elect,** Association of Black Queers Who Survived a Black Childhood, 2013–Present

SKILLS

» Hopping fences

» Hiding myself

» Development, including:

> » Giving false hope to people whose nation thrives because of their suffering

> » The "helping hands" of white people ($15,000 from forced allyship donations, 2020)

» Workshop facilitation and design (Topics: diversity as compliance, queer studies in the whitest way possible)

REFERENCES

» God as my witness

» The gay agenda

» Every person that's seen me cry

MY THERAPIST CALLED IT *CLIMATE DESPAIR*

& I'm having a hard time being perceived. In public,
I puddle into the nearest corner. In private, I fidget
my fingers as I cancel the 5th plan this week. There are
no commercials in the midst of burning. When I awoke
this morning, I told my heart to stop talking. Light
shone through my window & all 110 degrees were
the same thing. I walk to the store & a fight breaks out.
I walk back home & my mind goes missing. Dizziness pins me
to the pavement like Black folk when cop cars are too close.
There are no commercials in the midst of fat-backed TVs
playing me, losing consciousness, on loop. Heat follows me
to the ER like a name somebody else chose. Heavy eyelids
are insult to injury. Tomorrow morning I embrace
the hospital bed like isolation during the worst heatstorm
in history till I turn my head to mama. *Be lucky the laws were hot
or you would've burned to death.* There are no commercials
in the cartoon we call *U.S.* Remove the memorized
guide from my brain.

FUCK ME, JEFF BEZOS

Search All Departments ↓ : financial freedom						
Cause I can do all the tricks.	I can give you what Mackenzie (also call me) couldn't.	I can do a hand-stand, even in space, Jeff—I need you in me today.	My people got bills & ill will because of it.	The babies scam to get food in their bellies.	I will pretend to have a gender for you.	I will pretend it isn't fucked up what you did & do;
Compare similar items:						
I don't have to be more specific cause it all applies in this sentence;	Jeff, I could treat you real well.	I only want per year what you make in a day.	I could end hunger worldwide or buy myself a pair of shoes that doesn't talk back when I buckle them—	Please, Jeff.	I'll buss it down for a real crook.	I'll straighten up if a back arch & Plan B will fill my people's pantries—
Inspired by your purchases:						
They're hungry, Jeff.	I'm sub-missive & breedable—	turn me into a mule (with consent)—	mix your donkey with my horse—	you'll know what that means when you call me;	fuck me into being a single parent.	I'm wait-ing at my door in a housecoat, with a pen.
More items to explore:						
I'll raise them well, & away from you,	into a world with better ten-dencies.	One where houseless-ness isn't for sale on Amazon.	I think I love you too, Jeff.	I'm wish-ing we're in the same town for at least an hour soon.	I loathe the world enough to do it.	Even just for one night.

COGNITIVE DISSONANCE

On 11th Street, Saturday October 15th,
On a street with "Black Artists Matter" coloring the pavement,
& pillars with faces of renaissance-era Black artists
lift up the highway that tore the city in two,
& "Black lives matter" is embroidered in a local shop's window,

I see no Black people. Unless it is MLK Day,
or intentional congregations of underfunded Black events,
Black folk retreat to their faraway corners, speaking a variation of
the country's language that sounds like squeaking
styrofoam to those who populate 11th Street. My car glides

down a road where a venue, a member of the Chitlin Circuit
still stands only cause of national designation,
everything around it fresh as a new gun,
down a road where a monument honors—
through force—Black people in Texas. Down a road

where homies learned how to play ball, tie
their new Christmas shoes, live big despite the meager
bounties put on their heads by this city a century prior,
& it's nothing but white people. The internet says

In Austin, East 11th Is the New SoCo
My homies say *In Austin? Our lease is up in February*
What is a city if not a slowly rotating thing
baking its Blackness at the speed of capital? Every street,

in every city eager for all the wrong reasons,
reminds me of my skin. It isn't green enough.

THE MALE GAZE SERVES BLACK PEOPLE DINNER FOR ONCE

What they actually fear is mercy
said the Black boi at the all-white dinner table
We clink our glasses at the middle-grade novel release
at the nonprofit gala / at the function that was marketed
with all BIPOC on the flier / It's irksome
to exist atop the male gaze's fear / if mercy
means they cannot exist as the only thing sparkling
as the only thing worth aspiring to, screams
would follow / bullets would come hunting
the Queen of England would take America back
farther than a white girl cutting a Black man's hairline
Good thing they wouldn't let that happen / what's happening
in America's gaze is the crinkling of a foundation / White people are
the only villains left / It's time to get my promise back
It's time to get your Timberland boots off the necks of people
you call *equal* / Men exist as if it doesn't irk me / I take Zoloft
so the depression isn't irking / Depression is a simpler way to say
dinner's ready, come get a piece of dark meat

AMERICA (REMIX)

A lake is just a lake, though people spent moons

drowning in spite of enslavement. A lake is just a lake

that drifted us from our homes & into the Stringer's Hotel.

They don't call it layaway anymore.

Instead it's 3 installations, rebranding kids wanting cool

plastic come Christmastime in the noonday

when everyone's wide awake; waiting on what we've

prayed for is the American way. Like I can BIPOC my roots

away from a plantation. Like all the white people saying

neighborhood improvement & *All Lives Matter*

when what we mean is we want you hot

& slaughtered in today's news Like

nudes slipping away from a cloud service. I *All Lives*

*Matter*ed my way to a gravesite. I lived to see

niggas blaming me for a capped skull outside a corner store

where cops loiter bloodthirsty for Black teens. I copped me

a *Reimagining Public Safety.* When you pinch its palm,

it says *maybe tomorrow.*

When grass eroding the middle of the concrete

tells me more about today's climate

than Joe Biden, & the news tells Palestinians wanting justice

 it's too complicated,

& colonization gets rebranded

for war, I must say I'm getting sick

of the bullshit.

A monument is a monument. I have no metaphors ready

for genocide today. I miss when *remix* meant my niggas

all on the same track, not a toy being dead

because you held it to the light.

NOTES AFTER WATCHING THE INAUGURATION

I walk campus and wonder if I'm standing
on an unmarked grave. Are we under
concrete, grass, or any other forced terrains?
I wonder again, this time, if *violence* is
a remix of what the making of America
is while white boys blare music, use
MAGA banners as decoration on white walls
down the hall from Starbucks. Is Starbucks
a stand-in for *brother*? Time is a mark
of body decay and not much else.

**

Before I was a poet, I was a lineage. One that
asked questions of diners when they didn't
let us in, one asking if I'd like my mocha
with the white chocolate as white girls
celebrate *victory*. Who wins when I decide
white. Before I was a human, I was free
which is the healthiest of human abstractions.
Free has the best marketing team. I am
the violence that forced itself into life.

**

In an alternate timeline, I was someone
with less life taken up by what kills me.
More sure I had a home, its history
singed in paneled pink walls. Sure
that it was mine & safe to dance in;
I was happier here, since there are

no inaugurations. There are no cameras
capturing my ending.

**

At protests, I see them with their cameras.
They snapped faces of weary elders
in their cameras. They got BLM as hashtag,
Blackness as temporary and distant
in their cameras. Can they, through bright
silence and access to hope, see me through
their cameras? They got the whole wide world
watching us perish. They got the whole wide
web in their terror-lens.

*Turn off your Wi-Fi. Bring plenty
of water. Wear masks & gloves;
get up when they spray you.
Call for help, call for anybody
but them. Singe contacts on
your skin. They get mad when they
can see your camera. If you listen
to the chants enough times,
you'll catch on perfectly. Broken hearts
in unison sound easy, like doomsday.*

**

When the white folk come for me,
When the state troopers come for me,
When the graveyard comes for me,
When the Starbucks comes for me,
When the cameras come for me,
When Republicans come for me,

When Democrats come for me,
When my own demise comes for me,
Who will answer the door?

**

This is not my house. Someone else
must open it.

I'M NOT WRITING ANYTHING ELSE WHERE WHITE PEOPLE ARE THE ASSUMED AUDIENCE

forget the references forget the review panel full of wonderbread who've written metaphors
for my skin forget the handshake forget friends who only reference other wonderbread friends
forget feeling bad for never finishing an episode of *Friends* forget the discourse & allyship forget
wanting the revolution's sides to be more diverse forget converting the 50sum percent of folk who
still think they aren't racist forget the 50sum percent of folk who still think they're antiracist
forget the nuance & sparing their feelings with every line & stanza forget "show, don't tell" for
niggas in single-file lines for their lynching forget their desire their presence their hate mistaken
as healthy forget the unhealthy white girl berating me on the zoom call forget rage mistaken
as hate forget Defund The Police Is Not Realistic forget Nancy Pelosi & the police forget the
bombings & shootings & recanting all this shit so you can feel me less forget the stares forget
ignorance assumed of the reader forget mistakes forget writing more like them / to them / with
them / in spite of them forget white rage forget Black pain paraded as prose & poem I am writing
what Booker T needed all of this time I am writing for Phyllis for Sonia for Audre for James I am
writing a poem that I don't need to explain Let minstrelsy take its rightful step inside the trash
can Let the gaze of the white everything step away from my pages & my poems & my power Let
them be a choir of stares Reader I am writing this poem for me—

S.B. NO. 8: ERASURE

This piece is a poem derived from the original text of Texas Senate Bill 8, passed on May 19, 2021.

BE IT ENACTED BY THE LEGISLATURE OF THE STATE OF TEXAS:
This Act shall

                                        criminalize abortion

Health and Safety   is amended

                                        as follows:
    "Fetal heartbeat" means

                            the human

                                    is carrying

                    calculated

judgment
    "Unborn child" means a

                    LEGISLATIVE
                        reach

    Texas has compelling interests

                in protecting the health of

_____

                to make an informed choice

                            is

not

        appropriate

        A

                pregnant [person]

is

        PROHIBITED

                a physician may not knowingly

physician

        This section

prohibits abortion.

this

                    shall make

the   [womb]

                              a medical emergency

                                             This
subchapter does not   recognize a right to abortion

      This subchapter may
authorize the
      prosecution of a [womb]
            a political subdivision
   prohibiting abortion   is
   law of this state.
      private civil actions
may be   threatened by
            any person
bring [un]civil action against any person who
      performs or   induces

                        abortion
the court shall award:
$10,000 for each

                  Civil Practice

                                    this
section

               is
      ignorance   ;

                        this
subchapter   unconstitutional;
      a defendant's
abortion

                              is

      affirmative
      a person
   performing or inducing the abortion   is

                              Affirmative
                  this state
                  may not intervene in

                    This

                            Procedure
                        Abortion
                            is
                            the right of

[those] seeking an abortion
    abortion

                                                Is
                                        relief

        is
constitutional

                                AND
                    valid
        valid

                            valid
                    valid
valid

                            valid
                        valid
            valid
                valid
                            valid
                    valid

III. BEDROOM

I ADMIT IT

I am not always hypervigilant
about killing bugs when they tangle
in my locs. I fart without turning
the other way so the smell is hostage

under the sheets while my partner sleeps.
I've done unspeakable things & here I am,
telling you so you can get on with it. I cheated
on a test. I cheated on a partner & talked

about her worse when she left. I watched a friend
be berated by homophobes & did nothing
but walk him home, in silence. I've been so silent

you could scream all year & it wouldn't be enough
to fill the blank spaces. On days where my limbs
are glued to the bed like stars in the sky,

I scroll until my eyes are tired
of dog pics & tragedies. Sometimes,
I don't repost the graphic with the hashtag.

Most times, I care less & less about the action plan
for freedom. You don't have to comment;
you don't have to convince the police.

They are already sending dogs for me. You don't
have to justify bypassing another mother's tears

for a formality—no *they should've complied*
needed. This is me coming clean. This is me,

turning my wrists to the whitest part for optimum
cuffing. Can you resist the urge to kill me?

It's true; I cannot kill a pig with my bare hands.
It's a hard rule to live by—not distancing myself from the terror
that brings me joy. I want to feel good after a meal
without the smell of death on my hands. After all,
the pig gives me so much
pleasure. Every morning, I wake up & offer
myself humanness. What does it mean to be human?
To be the opposite of a machine, of course.

I want to be as flexible as my glass-covered father.   Instead,
I bend to the mistake of the habitual; mess up   till
the messiness compounds into something I can't ignore.
I gave up womanhood to be a cyborg.   I want to be as impulsive
as a computer program—everything all predetermined & bending

to human   composition.   Every need thrusting into me
long enough to drain the womb from my palms. Let's continue   lubricate my vessels &
store my emotions   in a blender.   Pick   a task for me
to do over & over—   wash the dishes—   fetch the remote—

suffocate the girlhood from me—I'll shoot up
any microchip if it makes me into a god. The god that I know even said
I look more like him.

It's true. I cannot kill who I used to be   even with
technology. What does that mean for me then?

SPONDYLOLISTHESIS, OR WHY I EAT TACO BELL

I grab a #7 when I'm most depressed. Like today,
scarfing down a Crunchwrap Supreme to drown out

the dagger & twist in my lower back. Like tomorrow,
the Baja Blast overpowering the Black boi asking

for anger to save them in my throat. My back hurts
in a country that wants to disable me. What feels

better than hard-shell medicine, a lover (read: stranger)
asking if you need anything else. So I stuff my sadness

with hot sauce packets. My gifts come wrapped
in hexagons too sexy for my pain. Weary needs saving

as much as it needs flavor & a country not cashing in
on Black suffering. What's your after-appointment fix?

Mine costs $7.22. Mine is fractures with enough
decency to come packed with straws and napkins.

What does your healing cost?

& WHAT IF I WASN'T

so *well spoken*. So put   together with just enough   filter
to sit in rooms   where I ought to be   my fakest   What if
I never knew the code   to the   switch   Would I be swerving
in a hooptie still?   I already   know   the answer.   They act
like they don't so I   button my bowtie   tighter I'm gettin' spit
on all these master's   tools I'm over   compensating on my
enunciation of *fixing to*.   Since when   are they *fixing to*
care if I die?
So what if I can   pick a dinner fork from whatever   is   the other
one   when I choke myself with it;   what if I wasn't
forced to be a fool   I would be somewhere
on a picket fence yelling   *take me to your river*   *I wanna go*
what if I wasn't   poisoned   with perpetual   dissonance—

I TAKE MY THERAPIST'S SUGGESTION & CORRECT
WORRYING TO CARING

Caring is surely what we were made to do. Like
          when I care so much that I need an Ibuprofen to care
for the next thing on my list. Like when my girlfriend
          doesn't text back for hours, though she said
that she was going to work 3 hours ago, and her shift lasts
          8 hours, like it does every day. When I care myself
to tears; that's when I feel my most human. I think,
          which is a treasure. Caring means that I can feel,
which is a curse. What do we do when caring
          is a danger to yourself and others? What do we say
when caring nips our tongue & turns
          sentence into *shut it all down.* I want to care
only when absolutely necessary. Yesterday, I cared
          so much that my brother won't speak to me.
I lose followers like time—only when I've cared too
          publicly. I care about myself & others, often. What
do you care about when it isn't in your control? What do
          you do when care glues your limbs to the bed
like stars, no matter the war-riddled sky?

T SHOT #6: A PARALLEL UNIVERSE

If I were a boy
is not a phrase I yell only when Beyoncé sings it.
I think heavily on the day the nurse instead said
it's a boy

while my mother was dizzy with ache, nurses
taking her away from it. I'd be
a strapping young fella. One with a father
giving me sturdy wisdom. I'd be given the talk about hoes
but be into boys with medium-ugly faces, blues

running through my veins like guitar strings kissing
Black fingers. Tall in my heart, this thought's taken up
so much space. As I stare into the dark I picture me,

laughing haughty at mortal beings for thinking
anything non-man of me. If I see

different-gender KB
in a Walmart, looking for Imodium
for some mundane ache,
I would wear that sucker out with the backside
his mama gave him for used headspace

on a world I had to will here
with secrets & stinging surprise
injected in a different thigh
every Wednesday at 5 pm

If I were a boy
I would know how to pretend better

SNAKE PLANT

I'm giving a chance to the parts of me that need
to come home. For you, my lover, the concubine
of my truths, I'll tell you one honesty: the snake plant's
need for water & the soil's need for fertilizer every 4 weeks.
I think to give myself that same treatment. I fail
much like the crumbles of roots that become unalive
when getting this plant over to the other pot. We all need room
enough for our greatness. You're doing great in some other city
& mine too while I wait for you to live someplace other than
my discomfort. I thought I would be done with it
by now, but I'll take a new leaf,
a new vase to put in some new peace.

I'm asking a question: why did you let me do it? Create
my loneliness, level its sincerity beyond belief, let grief
take over the bed & beg you to take me back?
Is it the mask or masculinity that did it? It'll always be me
making messy what was chalked dust to begin with
and you, saying *no* etched in the memory of my dreams.

If ecology did a versuz against man, ecology would eat him up
every day of the week. I can't believe some of the things
I've been able to get away with. Cursing you. Badgering you.
Calling to say *I'm ready to get back together*
& you would've too if stronger influences let up again.
The snake plant's multitudes of brown flakes caked up
in its highest straightened leaves are a sign of decay.
You'd want to clip them if they got cancerous.

By my TV, it's grown from ankle-size to God.
It stretches its fingertips like second-graders
overcompensating for their height. I do that too while picking
white mulberries from trees on our neighborhood walks.
I feed them to you with stems still attached because your eagerness
to kiss the earth stump's dirt-flavored seeds. The snake plant
's grooves also remind me of your hips moving like water
to Bad Bunny, bare-faced & singing translations in my ear.
Funny: something can sound beautiful and mean *fuckboy*
in another language. Funny: you let me into you like love
living through the snake plant no matter my sometimes-neglect.

FOODIE, OR I MISS EVERY HOMETOWN COOKOUT

Fuck the presentation, I want the food to taste good. Like chopped

slop covered in barbecue sauce brisket. Like mama's wing flings

on top of greasy paper towels with a side of somewhat burnt

sweet potatoes. I want the meal to give me itis I can feel in my tongue,

tums needed to hush up the organs telling me I've made mistakes today.

None of it was a mistake, really. The only thing I regret is not asking

for extra hot sauce, extra communion with my niggas over hot plates

while barbed off in backyards with an uncle that has bunions on his toes

hollering CAN YOU HEAR ME under the bengay. Today, I hear you, auntie.

Swearing I forgot to take the chicken out; making chitlins in a room full of people

with my blood or at least best interest in their hearts. I say your name,

spaghetti & fish after a friend has went to pasture. I say your name as I look

at the coffee shop menu, wishing it had some spirit on it.

GOOD GRIEF
after Texas Winter Storm Uri

I'll admit that I've never thought about frostbite.

Trauma of the blood, a thing to be avoided when heat goes out for an entire state.

I don't know where to place this grief, this sweltering state freezing, politicians breezing over to a country that doesn't have tissue choked out by its winter yet.

The sky can only do what it does.

The American government can only do what systems driven by green paper, violence, & ache can do.

The trees bloom over dead bodies, missing.

The sound of hands rubbing, engines purring, hopes that gas lights or chafing or the rapture won't come first may quiver in my blood forever.

I am Black, & maybe I am doomed.

Memory flashes like a computer screen; I see the Zoom link expand. Colleagues process whatever failure number of a thousand this was this year & I can only remember white.

Six inches deep, sunken into my boots all over.

The timeline of friends stranded, impending doom of electricity shutting off, water pressure slipping into nothing every hour, pipes bursting on top of all that white.

I haven't recovered from seeing things that too closely resemble holes in a graveyard.

I haven't forgotten the project is due in 2 weeks.

My therapist says *take it easy* as if capitalism is listening. As if the body will ever forget what it is given.

I am Black which is history, personified.

I used to listen to "Pilot Jones" fondly. With all this frostbite on my fingers, I'm not sure if I can type.

I cannot finish another sentence on unity.

What is unified about ERCOT letting us freeze? Knowing how to fix the problem & not doing it; how does that form a Kumbaya circle?

If I made art about every pain I've felt unjustly, I would be swimming in accolades for great American books.

I would take back every word I've written if it ended this.

the U.S. is the worst group project.

I'm writing a great American poem about suffering.

How much is going without food that isn't canned for a week worth?

The absence of snow feels like betrayal. My memory mixes with American delusion.

I can't believe half the things that I've been through.

Ice cold, baby, I told you; I'm ice cold.

Who said it first, Frank Ocean or Christopher Columbus?

I've never been taught how to adequately mourn the nights spent bitching about a brisk wind; the night we almost got stranded trying to get to J before the cold swallowed them whole.

I want to give everything I've been handed a good cry. Red skin & chapped lips deserve it.

Good grief, what has Texas done to me.

An article features a person walking past tents near I-35.

I can't cry about the body but I feel it.

A highway splits a nation from its promise to be *one*.

Everything feels blurry and the palm trees have died.

Everything transported here withers away eventually.

6 months later & I haven't been able to shovel out my sadness.

A news report said that it's safe to go back to work. & I listen, because what else can you do in 6 inches of white.

The snow melted & I still feel frostbitten.

There are no heroes in a freeze-frame changing nothing.

I pose begrudgingly. Say cheese & then write this.

I'm not a survivor; just still breathing.

I remember grief, love's grand finale.

What else do we have if not the memory of life?

I cannot tell you how many lives I've lost to mourning, but I can tell you that the sky does what it does.

Let's go for a walk & touch the trees that survived like us.

Let's write a future more joyful & less inevitable in segments of leaves.

Anything we dream will be better than this.

SELF-PORTRAIT AS A HACKBERRY TREE

I latch on to unusual surfaces.
You call them buildings, I call them men with
handlebar mustaches. They protrude through & under
my meaty, barked-up branches. They try & cut me shorter
with instruments not strong enough for roots. I once broke through
what called itself pavement, too. & it felt good, telling him I didn't notice
the obstacle & stumbled my way through it to get to a land with healthier
terrain. I am a living invasion of the ecosystem's status quo. I thrive
with little more than sunlight & air protruding through my
already-watered roots. How good it is to be bumpy
but keen on survival. It's nice to meet you
on both sides of a fence.

AFTER BINGING MAY I DESTROY YOU IN 3 DAYS

Multiple things can be true at once. Like me,
still messing up the title of this show & it being
the best thing I've witnessed in years. Like me,

being a survivor, still being scared to say
the word *rape*, & it being the defining
experience of my 20s. Would you believe me if

I said there's life to live after loss? Would it
make sense to be serious yet less sympathetic
after a 40-minute episode you have to talk about

in therapy? Before I was a survivor, I couldn't
have been a woman. Before a tree drops its first set of acorns,
some are already considered

rotten. Before I had *queerness* I was a kid, waiting
on all restroom stalls to be vacant before exhaling.
I remember nothing but the feeling after that forced,

compliancey apology. *Hurt people hurt people*
is a really weird way to say rape. I remember ditching
the scene, humming the anxiety away with a song. Maybe MAY

I DESTROY YOU feels more accurate to the experience.
The song in my most haunted memories sounds like
better run / to the ark / before the rain starts.

FLEETING THOUGHTS ON A DEADNAME THAT'S NOT QUITE DEAD

Indignant, I demand the panelists say my name.   I'm begging my psyche
to let me tell homies   my new name. I put up with   a name

because it feels too much   like home. New friends dap me up,
in crowds of people, call my name.   The cashier can't hear me   when I yell
it isn't hard to correctly   *spell*   *my name.*   Two letters of
secrecy;

one for knowledge,   one for fame.   Baseline,   it is my only name.
I can't say it any clearer.   In the mirror   I do not see

a name. I see a face with many visions   of hearing my name different.
I hope my lineage   knows I'm respectful   of the name
they've given.   On legal papers I'm ignorant

to what I see on the page.   Say my name   Say my name
but only if you let it change
for me. I'm dead   as in I don't live for you   anymore. I birth myself

into   my own
name.

SIN CITY

after Carrie Fountain

I'm tired of taking orders, answering
phone calls, wasting time
sweeping floors that aren't mine,
working for daniel/david/lester, being annoyed
by becky/lindsey/heather, getting all my customers stolen
cause I'm not the pretty girl at the bar,
leaving clues like an amateur sleuth
that I don't want to be here,
going to/leaving work broke—I'm just tired.
Tired of telling trauma *not today, Satan.* Telling grief
and depression *not today, Satan.* Telling being
human and feeling *not any day but especially not*
today. I'm tired
of being the Black person in your workshop/workplace,
tired of teaching how not to be racist/sexist/stupid,
tired of talking when no one's listening and shaking
my head to your senile status quo. In a perfect world,
I'd be somewhere away from here. Running swift
with my pink slip, ready to slit
anyone who dismissed me with heart-bleeding bliss
and sit in your white-ass classroom with a grin,
waiting on my turn to spit
my needed feedback on your Black poem,
not wondering if this
is where I'm supposed to be.
I'd finally have money to get my A/C fixed. Lose enough
for old jeans to fit, then get drinks at Stonewall to reminisce
on a time when I wasn't tired, and smoking weed/taking risks
were the only sins I embraced, heart full with love. Hands dripping
with possibility.

WHAT'S ON YOUR MIND, KB?

How much cloth & cotton & 2 stabs
of chemicals you can't name
saves you. Did Waffle House ever
shut down? Has anyone ever cared
about a stranger, or is care a man
-made abstraction? When I'm kissing
my partner, I'd like to focus on her
kissing me, not the redness ringing
on my ears from masking while asleep.
not the cop car yelling "be afraid" while flashing
U.S. red & blue; intrusive thoughts—
wondering if I'll fail at life, at staying
alive, at doing whatever *this* is—I want all of it
less present when my eyes close & her lips
meet mine. Clouds part above us & our tongues flicker.
I remember we're in an avoidable pandemic
& we live in a city with no care for our kiss.
My eyes force-open, the car has trouble
starting, the food is cold & hairy, the date is
over before it starts. I wonder if the businessman
next to us knows freedom. Is he freckled
& always frightened like me? Is He on earth
blending in with all the other devils
like COVID, & cops, & everything that got us in
this place? My partner puckers up
for a finale. A bug flies into my face
like there isn't all this room to roam. Cops exist
like there isn't all this room to love. I kiss her
cheek instead & say sorry.

T SHOT #7

When I think of women, I think of K's Black hair. Though store-
bought, it was laid as if it wasn't; her body flowed on dance floors
like shame wasn't a factor, as if every factor in the world didn't exist.

& then I think of existence. Do I deserve it after the things I did
to K? The deception, the dumping, the terror I scratched in her?
How trauma makes a broken record of us. How the boys did

what they did when I wasn't old enough to know they do whatever
they want to. How is this my first time bringing pen to paper? How *rape*
feels too explicit of a claim even 20 years later. I don't speak

to K anymore, but I do flinch when lovers trust in me too much.
I fear that the breaking will turn into wounds I go to therapy
for. And then I think of all the sessions I've spent

on K. When women in my life spend their labor on me—
my lover, my therapist, and K—I think of history. My growing
mustache doesn't mean I must repeat it.

IV:
LIVING ROOM

ARS POETICA FOR GRANNY

This is a poem that I hope hugs you
into a timeline where men
don't happen to us again

T SHOT #3: BLACK HAIR

burgeons through my pores
bringing its small, itchy sores. Cuts
through my hands and stubbles up
enough to be visible when fitted
skin-tight to a mirror. One day,
I was standing so close you could
see each pore & I'd pluck until
every red-and-Black follicle knew
no hair was welcomed here.
Now they sprout and I'm foolish
with joy at every conjuring of
a bush. Every prick rubbing
its way through my patchy
happy face. *Who will teach me
how to shave?* YouTube, I guess,
till my bois get this far. I wonder
if every beard grows like this: into
a nest made with oil and hope. Into
a boi made with oil after they threw
away the rope. I guess I'll put
that in the search bar too: *did it feel
good, to stop running from yourself?*

POETS ARE BETTER ~~AT EMPATHY/MORALITY/~~ ~~BEING A FRIEND~~ THAN ANYONE ELSE

is a lie if I've ever heard one. Poets are good
at writing with no rules other than feeling

a thing into being. Poets are good
at good fortune & ghosts. Good Poetry is nepotism

if I've ever seen some. When I think about poets,
I think of humans with their hair follicles & heart

in one hand, tiny TVs replaying everything
that's ever happened to them in the other.

Posterior is nothing in comparison to a poet.
This poet thinks outside the page is the work

that must be done. We ember & kindle
& nothing else. Poets are better at whimsy—

they echo every poet they've ever known,
but better at humaning? Not really. Is this a poem

or something stumbling out of me like legos
on a childhood floor? I don't know.

Better go ask a poet.

POEM AGAINST "BLACK _____ MAGIC"

after Hanif Abdurraqib

When James Baskett didn't win the Oscar for Uncle Remus &
Viola Davis did win the Oscar for Aibileen &
Hattie McDaniel did what she did & what Viola did to win these Oscars &
Will Smith didn't win the Oscar for Hitch—
it never was ~~his her~~ our Oscar—I started to believe our magic
came from the crack our back has to get
bending over continuously. They defined
what's good—what trophies & CV fluff was needed to be *prestige* &
we praised the Magical Negroes who wedged they way through

violence. This poem isn't meant to bash our elders.
The blank space in textbooks &
the blank space in Viola's regret &
the blank space in syllabi &
the inclusion of Sound of Music &
the blank bookcases of niggas overqualified
for white awards says enough.

This poem won't give magic a false definition. Only a new
standard for Black folk who fancy themselves
only when their boots are drenched in driveled licks. If white
people dictate magic, then it's Black magic. Not
Black girl magic &
Black boy magic &
no supernatural negro made themselves 2nd to a white dream
for this & no white director gets the Oscar
at the mercy of the academy for my divine powers &
what even is my power when whiteness eventually
wipes all of us out?

Who are you outside of the ~~everywhere~~

~~ominous~~
~~always calling us "magic" in efforts to unalive us~~
white gaze? You know what is my magic?

The clarity I feel after laying down for 9 hours.
The slam of a laptop when I've said "no" to working
one more hour. The feeling of falling apart
in the arms of someone that cares whether I thrive
or perish. Knowing that there's people who will make a stink
if whiteness unalives me. You know what is *magic*?
You being here after all these years of killing
us off—on- & off-screen. You feeling
the furthest away from any eyes, letting
all that ~~pressure perspiration precision~~
perfection go. Freedom is the opposite
of trophies given by white leaders,
so find it.

T SHOT #5: ODE TO MY SHARPS CONTAINER

Holder of loose blood. Taker of contraptions
I use when I'm brave enough to save myself.
Visual reminder that I can do it. Former container
of pickles so you smell like sour victory. Glass
house of my gender. Chest hair–maker.
Every interaction at the coffee shop, on the
phone with medical providers, every nervous
laughter after checking the sex on my ID
comes down to you. Ass hair–activator.
Restitution for a 20-year gap between
who I was & could be. Balding beauty. Conjurer of
my wildest dreams, ones I've dreamed since
I was 13. Activist. Advocate. Apt to be who believes
in me. Tallying up all my T, & all my bois who didn't
get to be boys. Heaven sent. Heaven's back door,
roping me up through the vent.

WHAT STILL LIVES

after Texas Winter Storm Uri

The leafless oak trees. The junipers hanging down, insisting
on being caught in my hair. The splintered leaves sagging
on red oaks choked by old Christmas lights. The hackberries,
perfectly aligned on the wooden pointless fence. What is a fence
but a boundary, but a harsh message to stay out? The ball mosses
outnumbering the leaves on the battered oak tree. The cacti, mostly
brown but still green in the middle. A fence with crispy shrub & crape
branches hugging it. Small trees that remind me of nights where I had
central heat. I am a descendant of logical Black folk that survived
illogical conditions centuries ago. & then again. & then again, I'm sitting
on the couch, sending texts to people I don't know. I check in
after an illogical winter storm asking *Are you okay* when I myself
haven't considered the question. They pillage the city like they pillage
the trees: up to make new boutiques & coffee shops. Up to make the best
barriers money can buy. My best barrier is the Black skin I wear
when carrying a city on top of me. I acknowledge this grief today.
The Mexican plum, still downturned but blooming does too.

ALMOST-DUPLEX

after Jericho Brown

If I am the worst, why does the universe keep blessing me?
Is it because my grandmother prays every night?

When my grandmother prays every night,
she calls me a name I've never known.

When faith felt dark & I didn't know myself,
I thought *surely god isn't sending her to voicemail.*

The voicemail I have now is a formality
for those that don't know me & my grandmother.

My voice tenors on stages brighter than the moon
standing cute next to gorgeous at midnight. My name

lays at bay while I wonder why
the universe keeps blessing me.

ANOTHER RELATIVE SAYS KB DON'T CALL & DON'T WRITE, AGAIN

Quiet as it's kept, you know a thing or 2 about guilt.
What it does in the bones of fast girls & Bible-raised
queer kids who come from families that don't
talk about it like they should. You'd call it
Holy Trinity but there's nothing holy about night sweats.
There's nothing anointed about guilt being

burned with weed leaves in the middle.
Dank isn't the word for it. More like *pow*
goes the natural order of things because the pastor's wife
said you were a woman. *Pow* is the other pastor's wife
mandating skirts because there was something too wrong
about you saying *Hello.*   *Fast.*

Like you wasn't slow as hell running from predatory men
& rumors spread by people you loved at reunions (how dare they
ask why you don't visit). Have they abandoned the crops,
attempted to pull decades-old roots they've planted in you?
You're a Hackberry now; you

can't be uprooted by bigotry. What?
Does the greenery disturb you too much? You know
the answer to the age-old riddle. When a tree falls
& there's no one there to hear it, it vibrates
in the key of *I'm out of town again.*
Have a good time, though.

DEATH BY RETINA, OR ____ GOES FOR A SWIM

With all my agony behind me, I go shirtless
to the pool. Through hundreds of puzzled
stares from children & whispers wondering
what _____ got out, I make the choice

to not say _____ in this poem. Instead, I acknowledge
the splash onto my face in the too-cold water & chuckle
at cissies slipping to view me on top of the moss-covered floor.

The kiss wetly planted on my partner's lips is a kiss goodbye
to the monologue telling me *cover it up*. I can't cover
up my _____ tendencies if I tried. I can't stay afraid

of people who don't know _____s like to go
swimming & wonder how many times a plane
has crashed, dishes have clashed with the ground

beneath them, children were left scarred
as adults gawked at the sight of my gleam.
I wonder how many times Tom's eyes bulged

as he ran into a closed screen door trying to kill Jerry
like cissies run into run-on sentences
misplacing their shame onto me. Death by retina
is a hell of a fear. It had me by the throat

for 20 years. I am a _____ in pineapple-covered trunks
that wants time to wade in my evergreen
sadness like everyone else. Contrary to popular belief,

we _____s do things when we're not lying

on our backs in your dreams. I wasn't born to be
your kid's first _____ spotted at the neighborhood pool

so keep slipping over my gender & watch out.
You are not the only toxic algae here.

ON THE DAY OF THE TRIAL BLACK AMERICA LOST, AGAIN

I'm ready for mimosas. I'm ready for your phalanges touching
dents in my lower back. I'm ready for wartimes, baby. The kind
where men stumble, drunk with moonshine & memories
that could cut glass if they had enough guts to be knives. I'm ready
to show you my most tongue-dampening salsa dance. Let's tumble
in the kitchen while Spotify shuffles tonight. Let's drown our tragedy
in bottles cheap & silly with headache-inducing relief—let's do this
till the next shooting, or winter, or lung-bursting disease
that raptures the world then grows feet & runs. Let's be kids,
getting jiggy with it in the moonlight while the moon is still visible
& the cop regime hasn't burst through. Let's hope when they knock
down the doors we're already killing it with our moves.
The carcasses left behind have the most soulful grooves.

AFTER THE 30TH PLAY OF MONTERO
(CALL ME BY YOUR NAME)

I am my wildest dream
& that's enough, said the toddler
I'm still nursing in my head. I'm raising
myself to be meek as a snake
choking out the nearest rodent for lunch.
Fuck anybody that wants to muzzle
my genius till it quiets—
that means mother's judgment needs to be
crated. That means
white supremacy needs
to ease its way out of my veins. I'm wringing
mine & my bloodline dry of it.
I'm letting my dreams be bigger
than lines drawn in sand
pretending to be concrete. This December,
hell will have to freeze over
& let me rest at Nas X's feet.
If I'm going, I'll be the next one at the throne,
thrusting & loving my way into it.
I am my sexiest manifestation, said KB
uncaging themselves to run.

I CAN RIDE MY BIKE WITH NO HANDLEBARS

Every day there is something bothering me,
begging me to be a poem. The leaf shavings
& dog hair decorating the dark wood floor.
The Cheerios progressing into sogginess the longer I try
to write me positively into this poem, the contraption trapping electrolyte
water with an orange tint, the condensation painting the inside of the bottle.
I'm seconds close to the ground at all times.
All it takes is a break

in the body's precision; a bruise is an imbalance
of inertia coupled with the gaudiness of men. No one can tell me otherwise.
I think I've muted the trumpets praising my eventual demise. In double time,
demons tell me I'm irredeemable, hastily laugh at all they've been able
to do to me and others. I've never been a gender.
Only a rhythm

building into chaos the more minutes are allowed to enter
this bridge. I can ride a bike, tell a lie, flip the leaf shavings
into joints that could trick suburban teenagers, trick the dog into thinking
I am the best human it's ever met, but what if instead I could live?
All I want to do is live! The chorus etches itself in red.
It reads *Learn forgiveness*
then you can lead a nation with a microphone
with a microphone
with a microphone—

HE/THEY IN THE STREETS, THEY/THEM IN THE SHEETS*

I do not dream of gender. Instead,
I dream that what's in between my legs
is not my destiny. Fairy.
Indie goth. I could be any
caricature. I do not dream
of expanding containers I never
actually purchased. Only no containers.
Only no dreams that see limits
on who I can be. Only Black queers
frolicking down the runway
next to all pronouns booked.
I wanna be booked for the next
flight. A one-way trip to freedom.

LOVE MACHINE

after The Miracles

All this time I thought we needed permission
to dance. Flap our imaginary wings. Schlep
sweat on our foreheads while making up moves
in every dance scene. My people are good at
dreaming up new grooves in the time it takes
one foot to pick itself up on the soul train.
We are love machines, unable to work for anybody
but rhythm, its everyday insistence on giving us
hope. No wonder why we can see a world without
police. Every day we smash badges under our busy
-good feet. We were made to see everything
beautiful before it hops & skips out of us.

SHE WALKED SO I COULD SKIP & JUMP

after Mojo Disco

Praise to the studs-turned-bois in crop tops. To the queens
who crown drag or heels as their only heaven. Praise to Essex,
to Audre, to James & his gap tooth. To the gap I rocked as a youth
& the stud-turned-baby-mama who left Facebook for 2 years.

      Praise to these gods & their freedom to *be*
      when they safe enough. To the candy-painted Barbie plate
      from a brotha who loves to watch me twist. To the ladies
      who get to be ladies when

the streetlights & club strobes gleam. & boys with 2
bills & children asleep that come cooing
when they need something real. To those who carry

      my truth, I give praise, I give praise to the theydies
      & gentle-hims who taught me how to mandate some gawd
      -damn respect. I guffaw in baby's ear, tell her what

you taught me 'bout justice. How it can be a broadcast
or taste of safety between baby & our bed.
How it can seem non-negotiable, but women who come
behind me had to wish for it by singing into a kitchen window

      begging god to let their husbands stay away
      for many evenings. I praise you,
      sisters & otherwise, for this manhood—a weapon I use
      to wage love & lose seldom. I praise you, king

sissies I keep with me when I let the truth dance.
On the right night, she knows how to let loose.

TALES OF TACOBELLA, OR I LIVE ON LIKE BLACK ROCKSTARS

like the night I spent 2 hours in the Texas sun sweating A/C units from my pores / like waiting to rage with some teenagers dressed in Black with white boyfriends squinting in glasses on their leather leashes / like the door whooshing in cold hair & hitting the posse I thought was my posse in the face / like the tickets sweaty in our hands as the doorman scanned them / like Rico coming out after 2 hours of swag surfing & turning our heads side to side / like my camera getting unbelievably shaky from jumping up & down with internet friends / like the hoarseness after screaming & taking up so much of the audio in footage / like taco bell seeming tasty after 4 hours of sweaty belly-empty ecstasy / like the nigga who decided to mosh himself into a health hazard so Rico had to get offstage / like the quesadilla—so cheesy it spilled all over my daisy dukes / like my sticky skin / like skid-mark nail polish that started to fade away as the day happened / like tectonics / like BITCH I'M NASTY playing in my head randomly for weeks after / I like you like Tacobella misses the times when kids could just be kids & ditch school to see rockstars, heavy with bass & disguising feelings that felt like prayers to a place where we live longer.

FINALLY, A SLOW WEEKEND

after Jericho Brown

My god, we leave things green
& greasy, like hands after massaging
kale to make chips. We love in colors
so vibrant; papaya orange, bell pepper
yellow & red. I want you mixed up
in me—push the rainbow strap
to green—at all times, especially on days
when the table holds our feet,
colliding & clasping its tar-black grooves.
The Freedom House is one where you
& me can love with no capitalism
to trick into it. & this has no limit to night
-time; the only rhyme or reason
to the day is sunlight & the neighbors
retiring into their homes. Let's keep them
unaware of the sweat we leave
in the grass while fireflies beam.
Let's make the earth decay under the makings
of an ancient birth—so regal,
the purple ridges of the sky blush.
Remind me from behind whose body
is yours. Remind me of the night
even if temporary & fleeting.

TRAVELING TO A NEW STAR

after Lucille Clifton

It was November and I was making a cup of coffee. In it sat
speckles of amber—all aromas reaching for the ceiling & smelling
half true to its actual taste. I lost my best friend 2 weeks earlier.
With him went the only recipe that made coffee drinkable.
Unlike sorrow, grief gets truer when you feel it. I went to school
1 year later, and at night, the city reeked of Moscow Mules
and old coffee grounds. No matter the light outside,

whether the pits of summer or 5 pm during unforgiving winters,
I can count on the moon being true to every feeling. I read my birth
chart, and it is closer to true than I will admit. The word *Grief*
underestimates the feeling, but I swear this world is born in it.
My best friend was close to the truth, and we built an entire world of joy
with that. My best friend put me through a hell, but is also
heaven to me. What is your personal Hell? Vegas? Failure?

The arms of an anti-beloved? Until this year, mine was the act
of making coffee, but this morning I have a French press
and a new brand; with joy, things feel different. I cannot see God
if I cannot see my joy. I started with truth and will end with me
closer to it. Love is passion, and passion leads us to these stars.
My friend who was my sadness is the star I never knew

I needed. Today, I'll take what I have and turn it into
something beautiful. When pain is the only thing that feels true,
I ride the wave of the moon until it drops me off at a new, speckle-
filled home. Baptisms happen everywhere. It is January,
and I'm making a cup of coffee with my loved ones.
Won't you share this stargaze with me?

CORONOSOMNIA

after Shira Erlichman

In this one, I am a driver approaching
a car at the first sighting of an evening dawn.
There is worldwide unrest. There is a seminal
slacking of slumber I'm tasked with driving into.
I've been forced into different circumstances,
unforeseen by me but not unforeseen by any
savior. I am not the only one that needs saving,
& I bring this with me into the driver's seat & set
cruise control in while all of the perils in my world
are exposed. Fear, get in. Memories that I wish
weren't memories, get in. Human-induced pandemic,
get in. Every passenger is everything about me
that keeps me up at night. I see me,
sweetening into the nighttime silhouette; on this road,
minutes creep by as I do, slipping into sour & then
the unfortunate opening of my eyes. Gender
dysphoria, get in. I jump from bed & sins speak to me.
I dream awake & someone speaks to me. They say,
I won't put you through what you cannot handle.
They see the world for what it is: a microcosm of everything
I can choose to heal from. My spirit, my middle-
of-the-nighttime miracle. I must name the thing
in order to heal from it. Everything I've experienced
is everything I need to know. In the face of turmoil,
my stillness is midnight sleep medicine. I travel until
I see a light. In the morning, I unbuckle every
passenger and we walk the path chalked in names
that we remember, in names that I can feel with my feet,
in sand that kisses me in the middle of a yawn
that propels the day. I am more than my own afflictions.
I, & this world, am worthy of self-work and forgiveness. Amen.

T SHOT #8

Every Wednesday, me & the homies virtually lock arms, start

swabbing with alcohol & progress into our veins of tomorrow.

In the beginning, I'd like to think God created flaws. They must have easily

seen other possibilities coming. Gender isn't God's creation;

it's a flaw of snapshot-thinking systems. We transform into scifi antimatter,

picking on Decepticon with our pink-and-blue needles. A prick isn't so simple

when there's death on the other side. The homies say *you got this*

when I hesitate meant-to-be for too long. Every Wednesday,

me and the homies stick shift gravity. The only way we move is forward.

A LIST OF THINGS I WANT BEFORE THIS LIFE LETS ME GO

A house paid in full for Granny. A house with a dog for me & G. Tiny
chickens running around the love-stained grass. Instagrammable

interior decor. An omelet made from vegetables I harvested. Proof
of me playing drums, shirtless. Lightened scars & teeth & tongue-cheek dreams.

Toes that I'm not afraid of showing. Learning from nights I didn't
know myself well. To kiss a pseudo-stranger on the head in a drunk tizzy

again. To hug my nigga till she screams *can you stop eating me out?!*
again. A bookshelf leaning from the weight of my thoughts & prayers.

Mostly, honestly, forgiveness. A silly-ass case of plastic splashed with matter
of gold paint that says I matter. To matter to most people, eventually.

An orgasm that makes everything feel like it's breathing. An orgasm that makes
everything in the day possible. My mother's acceptance, though that is nearly

impossible. I don't have room on this list for the finite. A smoothie
from Soup Peddler anytime I want. An endorsement from Soup Peddler

& my mother. A house on the sun that isn't only a house. A day
where my biggest task is to give my lungs a pardon

for willing me this far. A win that is a win only for me. A me that is
the foundation for the house that holds freedom.

FREEDOM HOUSE MANIFESTO

leisure for the youth / housing for everyone houseless / fresh fruit in the trees & kitchens of every America / a belly full & living / land back—truly in its truest form / reparations for all the land & promise Black America has been stripped of since infancy of the states / no student loan debt / no credit system to keep us drowning / no inequity tolerated / inequity eradicated from every living system / no system but the body polyam with all parts of the ecosystem / no belly full of legislators telling it what it can & can't do / no unrest, no bloodshed in the name of liberty & justice / no police / no prisons / no barriers between people / no ICE / no $20k medical bill / no cancer / no breeding of dogs that don't belong together / no dogs that matter more to you than people / no police / no memories of being handcuffed in front of a crowd inebriated & confused / no tickets sent to my residence for a red light I ran to get from 9–5 to 6–9 / no police / no prisons / no running my fingers through my hair looking for justice / no world devoid of it / no crying mothers / no breaking news of crying / no other / no *vote them out at the next election* / no politicians clocking me more than stopping ERCOT from killing people / no people owned by the state / no Greg Abbott / no police / no Ted Cruz / no police / no Donald Trump / no terror that will not be named because what we've done to each other doesn't have one / it may be eugenics / it may be degradation / or stages, the only place where I can say these things & not sit sideways for the next frame / no framing me for my own murder & no police / The Freedom House is one we all live in & win / The Freedom House is one we all live in & win—

MANIFESTMANIFESTMANIFEST

I had the urge to write *lived* but my heart's beating present-tense. I've lived many lives depending on who you ask to tell it. My mom, granny, best friend, even K will have something different to say—is it consistent to give fractions of me to each loved one? I am a transformer shapeshifting into every situation. I think I'm ready to house myself outside of shame. We should always remember: I am a poet above all else. By *we*, I mean all the child-me's finally being told *"I'm sorry"* inside of me. I believe that my feelings will do numbers for your feelings, & my country, & my city & once the terrible news gets better we live,

& live,

& live,

& live,

& live,

& live,

& live,

& live,

& live,

& live,

& live,

& live,

& live,

& live,

& live,

& live,

& live,

& live,

& live,

& live,

& live,

& live,

NOTES & ACKNOWLEDGMENTS

"I Can Ride My Bike with No Handlebars" has language from the song "Handlebars" by Flobots.

"Sonic Symbolism" borrows its title from the podcast "Björk: Sonic Symbolism." The poem is also inspired by Brittany Rogers' poem "Pantoum for Postpartum."

"Finally, a slow weekend" borrows its first line from the poem "Foreday in the Morning" by Jericho Brown.

The poem "Almost-Duplex" riffs off a poetry form created by Jericho Brown called "Duplex."

* - Everytime you read this poem, donate (or tell someone to donate) to the Transgender Education Network of Texas. Their website is https://www.transtexas.org/

"She walked so I could skip & jump" borrows its title from a sentence first uttered by Mojo Disco on "Eat Pray Thot" podcast episode 321.

"Good Grief" has language from the song "Pilot Jones" by Frank Ocean.

"after binging MAY I DESTROY YOU in 3 days" has language from the song "It's Gonna Rain" by Rev. Milton Brunson & the Thompson Community Singers.

"& what if I wasn't" has language from the song "River" by Leon Bridges.

Many thanks to Sebastián Páramo, Will Evans, and the whole Deep Vellum team for believing in this book.

Thank you to the publications who gave poems in this book their first home, often in earlier drafts:
 » "A List of Things I Want Before This Life Lets Me Go" – *African Writer Magazine*
 » "& Somehow, Men Are Nicer to Me Now," "KB Goes Home for the Holidays," "Freedom House Manifesto" – *American Poetry Review*

» "T Shot #2" – *ANMLY*

» "T Shot #7" – *beestung*

» "Black Life circa 2029" – *The Cincinnati Review*

» "I Can Ride My Bike with No Handlebars" – *Cobra Milk*

» "Bare Minimum, or To-Do List for White America" – *Drunk Monkeys*

» "KB's Origin Story" – *Electric Literature*

» "Everything's Temporary" – *Emerge: Lambda Literary 2018 Fellows Anthology*

» "The pickup comes at 6 am," "I take my therapist's suggestion & correct *worrying* to *caring*" – *The Hellebore*

» "The Male Gaze Serves Black People Dinner for Once" – *Homology Lit*

» "T Shot #8" – *Hooligan Magazine*

» "Almost-Duplex" – *Interstellar Literary Review*

» "Black hair" – *just femme & dandy*

» "I'm not writing anything else where white people are the assumed audience" – *Kissing Dynamite*

» "T Shot #4" – *The Knight's Library Magazine*

» "Ars Poetica for Granny" – *the lickety~split*

» "T Shot #1" – *The Offing*

» "Foodie, or I Miss Every Hometown Cookout" – *Okay Donkey*

» "Sin City" – *Pamplemousse*

» "Finally, A Slow Weekend" – *Perhappened*

» "Notes After Watching the Inauguration," "My therapist called it *climate despair*," "Snake Plant," and "T Shot #9: Ode to My Sharps Container" – *Poetry Magazine*

» "I Admit It," "Death by Retina, or _____ Goes for a Swim," "Poem against "Black _____ Magic" – *Poetry Northwest*

» "Fleeting thoughts on a deadname that's not quite dead" – *Poetry Online*

» "Sexting at the Gynecologist" – *Poets Reading the News*

» "Curriculum Vitae," "Greedy Ghazal" – *Prolit Mag*

» "Self-Portrait as a Hackberry Tree" – *Protean Magazine*

» "Every Building in East Austin Is a Ghost," "It's 6 am & the Sun Is Out" – *QT Voices: LGBTQ Studies at The University of Texas at Austin*

» "What's on your mind, KB?" – *Rejection Letters*

» "Ars Poetica with Election Results Still in Limbo," "We Are Owed This" – *Stone of Madness Press*

- » "after binging MAY I DESTROY YOU in 3 days" – *SWWIM*
- » "Spondylolisthesis, or Why I Eat Taco Bell" – *Taco Bell Quarterly*
- » "What still lives" – *trampset*
- » "Dinner with John Cena on the Moon" – *wildness*
- » "Tales of Tacobella, or I Live On Like Black Rockstars" – *WUSSY*

"Traveling to a New Star" and "Coronosomnia" were performed on tape with First Baptist Church of Austin. "Good Grief" won the 2022 Academy of American Poets Treehouse Climate Action Poem Prize. "She walked so I could skip & jump" placed second in the 2021 River Styx Prize.

Thank you to ire'ne laura silva and Kallisto Gaia Press for green-lighting *How to Identify Yourself with a Wound*, which gave me license & confidence to fully focus on this book.

Thank you to PEN America, and specifically Jubi Arriola-Headley, Roya Marsh, Nefertiti Asanti, Kimberly Nguyễn, Adrienne Oliver, and the 2021 Emerging Writers Fellowship program staff for being the first champions of this book.

Thank you to Megan Thee Stallion, Kiese Laymon, Jericho Brown, Danez Smith, adrienne maree brown, The Real Housewives of Atlanta, *Scam Goddess*, *The Read*, *That's So Raven*, *Eat Pray Thot*, Ocean Vuong, Cyrée Jarelle Johnson, Fatima Asghar, Terrance Hayes, Frank Ocean, Rachel McKibbens, and Camonghne Felix, whose work I consumed while writing this book. Whose work has surely textured this book.

Thank you to Gabrielle Calvocoressi, Zoë Fay-Stindt, Cloud Delfina Cardona, Jo Reyes-Boitel, and other friends/mentors for being treasured editors of this book.

Thank you to Gaby for being Gaby.

Thank you for reading. May we build the Freedom House together.

Beowulf Sheehan

KB Brookins is a Black, queer, and trans writer, cultural worker, and artist from Texas. Their chapbook *How To Identify Yourself with a Wound* (Kallisto Gaia Press, 2022) won the Saguaro Poetry Prize, the Writer's League of Texas Discovery Poetry Prize, and was named an American Library Association Stonewall Honor Book in Literature. KB's poems and essays are published in Poets.org, *Huff Post*, *American Poetry Review*, and elsewhere. They have earned fellowships from PEN America, Civil Rights Corps, and Lambda Literary among others. KB's debut memoir *PRETTY* (Alfred A. Knopf) will arrive in May 2024, and they are a 2023 National Endowment of the Arts fellow. Follow KB online at @earthtokb.

Printed in the USA
CPSIA information can be obtained
at www.ICGtesting.com
JSHW051808100624
64551JS00012B/564

9 781646 052639